Just in Time
Devotions for Advent

Dcvid B. Whitlock

Parson's Porch Books

Just in Time: Devotions for Advent

ISBN: Softcover 978-1-949888-36-2

Copyright © 2014 by David B. Whitlock

All rights reserved. No part of this book may be reproduced or transmitted in any form or by any means, electronic or mechanical, including photocopying, recording, or by any information storage and retrieval system, without permission in writing from the publisher.

Unless otherwise noted, all Scripture quotations are taken from the Holy Bible, New Living Translation, copyright 1996, and 2004. Used by permission of Tyndale Publishers, Inc. Carol Stream, Illinois 60188

Scripture quotations marked "NKJV" are taken from The New King James Version, Thomas Nelson Publishers, Nashville, 1982. Used by permission. All rights reserved.

Scripture quotations marked "KJV" are taken from The King James Version, Cambridge, 1769.

To order additional copies of this book, contact:

Parson's Porch Books
1-423-475-7308
www.parsonsporch.com

Parson's Porch Books is an imprint of Parson's Porch & Company (PP&C) in Cleveland, Tennessee. PP&C is an innovative non-profit organization which raises money by publishing books of noted authors, representing all genres. All donations from contributors and profits from publishing are shared with the poor.

For Lori, who came back into my life, just in time

Introduction

For centuries Christians have been celebrating Advent (literally "arrival"). Advent begins fours Sundays prior to December 25, on the Sunday closest to November 30. Although there are four Sundays in Advent, there are not always four weeks. For that reason, this book includes devotionals for twenty-eight days to accommodate the reader on the years when there are four full weeks of Advent. In those years when there are less than four weeks in Advent, the reader can simply take in more than one devotional on some days.

Each day includes a Scripture, a devotional thought, a quote, and a short prayer. I hope this book will help you experience the presence of Christ as you anticipate the celebration of his arrival.

Unfortunately, too many Christians are so distracted by the flurry of activities leading up to Christmas that they don't really experience much of Advent and thereby miss the joy that is part of anticipating Christ. This is, after all, a season of contrasting emotions: We yearn for simplicity as we resign ourselves to living complicated lives, sing of peace on earth while warring within ourselves and with others, schedule time with people we haven't seen in months or years and then count the days until we are once again apart.

And activities plague us like fleas on a dog. "Perhaps I'll curl up by the fireplace and spend a quiet moment with Jesus," you may think. The inner taskmaster reminds you that you have a Christmas budget to manage, gifts to buy and wrap, social engagements to attend, and meals to prepare.

It's a season of emotional pushing and pulling resulting in ups and downs, stresses and strains, hustle and bustle.

But it was not so very different on that first Christmas, was it? What with the travelling to their ancestral home for a census ordered by an oppressive government, the impossibility of finding a room, the lack of help with healthcare during childbirth, what could be more stressful for people?

And today, like he did then, Jesus arrives just in time.

Today, we wait for Christ, even as he is here in this world filled with all its contradictions and exigencies.

In the anticipation of his coming, we experience his arrival.

Dietrich Bonhoeffer, while imprisoned by the Nazis during WWII, wrote to his fiancé of something he had learned from that horrid place:

"A prison cell, in which one waits, hopes, does various unessential things, and is completely dependent on the fact that the door of freedom has to be opened *from the outside* is not a bad picture of Advent."

In the very act of anticipating Christ, he is already there, opening the door of your heart so you can walk freely with him hand in hand this Advent Season.

Day **1**
Just in Time

> *⁴ But when the right time came, God sent his Son, born of a woman, subject to the law. ⁵ God sent him to buy freedom for us who were slaves to the law, so that he could adopt us as his very own children. ⁶ And because we are his children, God has sent the Spirit of his Son into our hearts, prompting us to call out, "Abba, Father."--Galatians 4:4-6*

"Thank the Lord. You arrived just in time."

I had promised I would pray for his wife before her surgery. He was nervous for her, and I understood why: The surgery involved a complicated heart procedure. He requested that I, his pastor, be there.

But a car accident had delayed traffic.

I walked briskly into the waiting area, explained to the nurse my plight. She knew my friends were waiting and ushered me into the pre-op area where I was able to pray with her just before they whisked her away to the operating room.

Sometimes it seems like God is late, or maybe worse, has forgotten us altogether.

Unlike me on my way to the hospital, circumstances don't delay our heavenly Father. He is after all, the sovereign "traffic controller."

The Bible says it happened "when the right time came." What happened? God chose to send his Son to redeem us, that is, to buy us back and set us free as his sons and daughters. Not only that, he sent his Spirit into our hearts so we could cry out in an intimate relationship of love, "Abba," ("Daddy")[1].

It was the "fullness of time." People were tired of the Greco-Roman world's cultic gods; many Jews were looking for a spiritual freedom the Law couldn't provide; both Jews and Greeks were hungry for a religion that would meet them at their point of need.

Roman roads provided the avenue for the spread of the Good News; the *Pax Romans* (Roman Peace) established stability for the evangelization of the Empire; the Jewish synagogues furnished a place for Jews and Gentiles alike to encounter the gospel; and the Greek language presented a common *(koine)* means of communication.

If you're wondering why God hasn't answered that prayer or placed you where you think you should be, take heart: He knows your situation and what's more, he is in control. The right time is his time. Stay faithful.

The time was right.

The eternal God arrives in the incarnate Son, just in time.

He still does it today.

"God is never late, seldom early, and always on time: his time."
--- (Unknown)

Father, I'm grateful I can call you Abba. I trust that you will show up, just in time.

Day **2**
Troubled Prayers

> ¹⁵"LORD, look down from heaven; look from your holy, glorious home, and see us.
> Where is the passion and the might you used to show on our behalf? Where are your mercy and compassion now?" ---Isaiah 63:15
>
> "Oh, that you would burst from the heavens and come down!
>   How the mountains would quake in your presence!" ---Isaiah 64:1

As we begin the journey of Advent, it's sometimes difficult to "to get into it." Life is like that in many ways, isn't it?

I have a goal of exercising three to five times a week, but I don't particularly want to. I trudge up the stairs to my exercise room and do the workout routine anyway.

Today I'm supposed to be on the way to Christmas, but I can't seem to get my feet moving in that direction. It seems like an uphill journey; I don't even feel like getting ready to get ready.

And yet I know how much I need it.

Isaiah probably didn't feel it either. It seemed God had forgotten his people. Outside forces threatened to destroy the once mighty city of God. In the midst of his distress, Isaiah cried out to God. Speaking on behalf of the faithful remnant, Isaiah asked God to show mercy and compassion. The prophet longed for the day when God would show up and make things right.

But Isaiah and the people of God had to wait. And so do we; it's part of what Advent is about.

We wait.

After I exercise, I enjoy that feeling that comes with the accomplishment of a goal. I tell my wife that though I didn't want to work out, I feel better after I'm finished.

So, perhaps the place for me to begin the journey is where I am, for I can be nowhere else. I tell God how I feel, asking him to renew my heart. And my waiting isn't passive. As I choose to exercise the spiritual disciplines that bring me closer to Christ, I trust that God's grace will abound in me all the more.

And so I wait. Christmas doesn't come at once. I move in that direction anyway. As I do, I sense his presence. He is walking with me, tiny step by tiny step.

"Beloved, now is the acceptable time spoken of by the Spirit, the day of salvation, peace and reconciliation: the great season of Advent."

---Charles Borromeo, Archbishop of Milan, 1564-1584

Lord, I humbly ask you to renew a steadfast spirit within me, giving me a heart that longs for your coming.

Day **3**
In that Day

> *"But in that day, the branch of the* LORD *will be beautiful and glorious; the fruit of the land will be the pride and glory of all who survive in Israel."--- (Isaiah 4:2)*

My wife, Lori, and I like watching the evening news together. I've noticed a pattern in the programming. The first ten or twelve minutes of the news is devoted to "breaking" events, that is, what's most pressing, according to the newscasters, in world news. Usually this part of the program brings disturbing news. There might be a crisis in the Middle East, an economic debacle, a new health risk, or a catastrophic weather pattern.

Then, later in the broadcast the newscasters report on something brighter, perhaps a personal story about someone surviving a near tragedy or something positive someone has done for someone else.

The newscasters know we don't want to hear only doom and gloom; we long for good news too.

Isaiah lived in a trying time. It was like the first part of the newscast.

He saw things from God's perspective: The popular religious festivals were a sham, for show only; the people were rebellious in their heart, despite the outward appearance of propriety.

The nation was in turmoil, Isaiah tried to warn.

Then Isaiah looked beyond the disobedience of God's people to a vision of good news, a time of glory, a future time when Jesus Christ (the Branch of the Lord) would reign.

Today, we look back at the first coming of our Lord. We know that event, whereby God came to us, changed everything, even as we look forward to his second coming when he will ultimately establish his throne in the new heaven and new earth.

In this in-between time, when the news is often bad, we look back with faith even as with that same faith we anticipate a new and better day.

After all, the best part of the news is yet to come.

"In his first coming our Lord came in our flesh and in our weakness; in this middle coming he comes in spirit and in power; in the final coming he will be seen in glory and majesty.
---St. Bernard of Clairvaux

O Lord, I look back to your first coming and am awed by the very thought: You became one of us. And by your death and resurrection, you have given me the opportunity of life eternal. Keep my eyes on you as I anticipate your return.

Day **4**
Only Trust Him

> "This is how Jesus the Messiah was born. His mother, Mary, was engaged to be married to Joseph. But before the marriage took place, while she was still a virgin, she became pregnant through the power of the Holy Spirit."--- (Matthew 1:18)

Get the picture: Mary, perhaps as young as 14 or 15, realizes she is pregnant. She tries to explain it to her mother: "But I've never had sexual relations. I promise." And then she tells her fiancé, Joseph. What will he do? And what were they to say to family and friends? "Mary is pregnant, but she is still a virgin, in fact, she will give birth to the Son of God. She is supposed to name him Jesus."

Can you imagine the awkward silence, the whispers, the innuendoes, and the ridicule?

Naturally, Mary was confused. "How can this be?" she asked the angel Gabriel, who gave her the news. When he told her the Holy Spirit would come upon her and that she would give birth to the Son of God, her response is one of trust: "I am the Lord's servant. May everything you have said about me come true."--- (Luke 1:38)

Joseph also demonstrated trust for he did as the angel commanded and took Mary as his wife.

Had they not trusted God with what appeared to be impossible, there would be no Christmas story as we know it.

Are you at a place where God is asking you to take a step of faith? Part of growing as a follower of Christ is taking steps of faith. It's frightening when we don't know exactly where he is taking us or how it will turn out. In the natural, it is impossible. But with God, all things are possible.

That's what Gabriel told Mary: "Nothing is impossible with God."--- (Luke 1:37)

Take that step today and watch God work.

"If I had it all to do over again---I would have trusted Christ more."
---Henrietta Mears, at the end of her remarkable life of service to Christ, quoted in John Ortberg, *If You Want to Walk on Water, You've got to Get out of the Boat* (Grand Rapids, MI: Zondervan, 2001), p. 88.

Lord, my natural inclination is to shy from you when you ask me to take a step of faith. Instead, may I recall your actions in my past and in the lives of others? Knowing that you love me and won't let me fall, I reach in your direction.

Day 5
What Kind of Messiah?

> 4 Jesus told them, "Go back to John and tell him what you have heard and seen— 5 the blind see, the lame walk, the lepers are cured, the deaf hear, the dead are raised to life, and the Good News is being preached to the poor. --- (Matthew 11:4-5)

Many of the Hebrews anticipated a Messiah who would judge the wicked and reward the righteous. When Jesus took the Good News to people whom the religious folks deemed unacceptable, they couldn't understand such a Messiah, so they rejected Jesus.

Even John the Baptist apparently struggled with the kind of Messiah Jesus turned out to be. From his prison cell, John sent word to Jesus, "Are you the Messiah we've been expecting, or should we keep looking for someone else?"--- (Matthew 11:3)

Jesus' message was more about the forgiveness of sins rather than judgment of them. A time of judgment would come, just not yet.

Is this our struggle too?

I wonder if we gloss over the Messiah who was born to a family with meagre means in an out of the way place, a Messiah who inaugurated his ministry with a message of hope for the poor and powerless. Do we instead create a triumphant, conquering Messiah who rewards the righteous (us) while condemning the unrighteous (the people we don't like or look down upon)?

Today, Jesus is searching for evidences of Christlikeness in us. He's looking for things we do that make him smile, things like visiting the prisoners, sharing bread with the hungry, clothing the naked, extending a hand of grace to the outcasts, the unacceptable.

During this Advent season, be intentional. Make it a priority to do something for someone that you would not naturally or normally do. Maybe it's working in a soup kitchen, or sharing a meal. Perhaps it will be buying clothes for someone in need or visiting the lonely.

How will you know what to do? Look at the kind of people Jesus went to and go and do likewise.

"No one can know what goes on in the soul of an afflicted person. No one can know what secret inner ripening can come from suffering and sorrow. All we can know is that every individual's life is priceless---that each is dear to God."

---Christoph Probst, in "A Noble Treason"

Father, give me the eyes to see those you want me to touch. And let me reach out to them in actions of love, just like your Son did.

Day **6**

In His Time

> *Then God will establish one of David's descendants as king. He will rule with mercy and truth. He will always do what is just and be eager to do what is right. --- (Isaiah 16:5)*

I want to know when and where.

"Should we buy new appliances?" I ask my wife as she inspects a new refrigerator, oven, and dish washer at an appliance store. "What if God leads us to another ministry that requires us to move?"

It would be nice if God would send me a text message: "You will be in this location for five more years, so go ahead and purchase new appliances." Or, "In five months I am sending you on a new mission. Get ready, and by the way, don't purchase those appliances."

God doesn't work that way. We have to walk by faith and do the best we can in the circumstances we are in. But, this is the way we come to know God's ways because we have to trust him with our unknowns.

Some people become obsessed with the end times. Current events---especially in the Middle East---are interpreted as signs that Armageddon is fast approaching. Some books even provide maps to show how and where the final battle will be fought.

It's all interesting, but I can't imagine how one would arrive at these theories by simply reading the Bible without preconceived notions about the end times.

The people of Jesus' day also had a vision of how the Messiah would come and what kind of kingdom he would establish. Because they were locked into that vision, they missed him and his kingdom when he did come. Jesus grew so frustrated with the religious crowd that at one point he prayed: "O Father, Lord of heaven and earth, thank you for hiding these things from those who think themselves wise and clever, and for revealing them to the childlike.---(Matthew 11:25).

Don't expect God to reveal all the details of your future, much less where and when our Lord will return.

And that's okay. We walk by faith, a faith that opens us to his touch in the here and now.

"His final coming is like his first. As holy men and prophets waited for him, thinking that he would reveal himself in their own day, so today each of the faithful longs to welcome him in his own day, because Christ has not made plain the day of his coming."

---St. Ephrem, from a commentary on the Diatessaron

I long for you, Lord, right here, right now. It's the only place I can experience you, for it's where I am.

Day **7**

Waiting on God

*Show me Your ways, O Lord; Teach
me your paths.
Lead me in Your truth and teach me,
For You are the God of my salvation;
On you I will wait all the day.---(Psalm 25:4-5, NKJV)*

I remember watching my older brother, Dougie, getting ready for school when he was in first grade and thinking, "I can't wait to go to school."

Then when I was in school, I recall saying, "I can't wait for recess," or "I can't wait for summer."

And so it went: I couldn't wait to move up from elementary school to junior high and junior to high school and then to college. I couldn't wait to start a career and family. More recently, I couldn't wait for my first grandchild to be born. So much of life is spent in an "I can't wait" mentality.

I understand the drive to move on. And that's not a totally bad thing. There's nothing wrong with wanting to improve, advance, and stretch.

But if I'm not careful, I miss what's happening in the present moment because I'm anxious to go forward.

I've found solace in the prayer of David. He waited, "all the day," on the Lord.

I start my day by vowing to wait on the Lord and not make decisions apart from seeking him and his will. But I'm often tempted to move on, with or without God. I have to remind myself to take one day at a time. David said he waited "all the day" not "days." Thinking of all that's before me is overwhelming and makes me anxious. I can only wait one day at a time.

If there is ever a time when I hear that phrase, "I can't wait," it's during the Christmas season. The kids "can't wait" for Christmas day, and often the adults "can't wait" till it's over.

Advent reminds me to be intentional in my waiting on God. Learn to wait on God---not just for the big decisions like a career choice or whether to get married or remain single, but for the seemingly small stuff too, like what to purchase for Christmas, whether to take some time off, or what to say to a discouraged friend.

As I wait on the Lord, I discover he is already here.

"How much of human life is lost in waiting?"---Ralph Waldo Emerson

"Lord, remind me that when I wait on you, you are able to show me your paths."

Day **8**
Just say "Yes"

*"Oh, how my soul praises the Lord.
How my spirit rejoices in God my Savior!"--- (Luke 1:46-47)*

So much mystery surrounds Mary, the mother of our Lord Jesus. How does a 15 year old girl prepare mentally to give birth to the Son of God? The Scriptures indicate she struggled with the news that she, a virgin, would give birth to a child. Did she strain to understand the boy Jesus as he grew? What did she tell him about the time the angel Gabriel visited her?

One thing we know for sure: Mary had a heart for God, for after initially questioning Gabriel, her response to him was a resounding, "Yes." As frightened as she must have been, she trusted God. And in that trust, was the "Yes."

We fear what God has in store for us when we don't trust him. Think about it: If you totally trust God with your life, you can step out in faith, daring to dream big dreams, willing to venture into unknown places and uncertain situations because you know God is a God whom you can trust...totally.

So often, we're like the little girl on vacation at the beach afraid to swim in the ocean. The father tells her he will be there, right beside her. He describes how fun it is when the waves gently lap over her, how he will teach her to float and play water games with her brothers and sisters.

But she resists.

Finally, on the last day of the vacation, she ventures out and to her joyous surprise, she discovers Daddy was right. She loves it.

Then she begins to cry. "What's wrong?" Daddy asks.

"I wish I hadn't waited until the last day of our vacation to get in the water."

God has an adventurous life ahead for you. He has promised never to leave or forsake you. But, to enjoy this wonderful, albeit mysterious life, you first have to say what Mary said to God the Father, "Yes, Lord, yes."

Will you?

> "Strength of my heart, I need not fail, Not mind to fear but to obey,
> With such a Leader, who could quail?
>
> Thou art as Thou wert yesterday.
> Strength of my heart, I rest in Thee,
> Fulfil Thy purposes through me."
> — Amy Carmichael

Lord, I want to say "Yes," to you today, right now. Help me in my weakness to lean on your strength and receive your "Yes," to me.

Day **9**

Christmas in July?

Oh, how my soul praises the Lord.
How my spirit rejoices in God my Savior! --- (Luke 1:46-47)

My wife occasionally breaks out in song when it's just the two of us at home. "You have a really good voice," I compliment. "You should be singing in the choir."

She disagrees: "My voice isn't that good. Remember, I didn't even make the Varsity Choir in high school."

I think she's improved.

I recall hearing her singing some months ago. It was July, in the heat of the summer.

She had the pitch and the words down pat, but something was just not right.

The song, "O come, O come Emmanuel," seemed out of place.

"Isn't that a Christmas song?" I asked as I peeked around the corner.

"Yes."

"Why are you singing a Christmas hymn in the middle of July?"

"I like the song," she answered.

At least she wasn't trying to spiritualize her way to a Christmas in July sale.

Christmas doesn't have to happen only in December.

So I asked myself, "Why can't my wife sing a Christmas song in July?"

She's not rushing the season; she's enjoying the presence of Christ as she sings.

After all, the hymn writer wrote the words, "O Come, O come Emmanuel."

If Christ can come to an out of the way country like Judea in an obscure place called Bethlehem, surely he can come to you when you sing about it in July or any month of any year.

And you don't have to have a Christmas in July sale as an excuse for your carol.

And ransom captive Israel
That mourns in lonely exile
Until the Son of God appear
Rejoice! Rejoice! Emmanuel
Shall come to thee, O Israel"

---first two stanzas of Latin hymn "O come, O Come Emmanuel" translated by John Mason Neale

Lord, open my heart to your coming any season, any day, and when you do, let me rejoice, singing a song of love to you.

Day **10**

Pay Attention

"Please listen to me."--- (Genesis 23:11)

Have you ever had difficulty finding the right gift for someone? Perhaps you've thought it over and over and still can't come up with the gift you want for that particular person. In some instances the best thing you can give is the gift of your own self. More than anything else, what some people want is your attention. Perhaps it's someone in a long term care facility or a person confined to their house. It could be one of your parents, grandparents, or a child.

I made a commitment that on Wednesdays I would visit long term care facilities and the detention center. I sometimes say that on those days I visit those who can't go anywhere. f I ever have to miss my Wednesday visit, they let me know it the next time I'm there. I often hear them say when I arrive, "I was hoping you would come, I missed you last week."

Advent would be an excellent time to visit some of those folks in places where they can't go anywhere. Pay attention to them. Look them in the eye and listen to what they are saying and not saying.

And if you are in a situation where you are confined to one place, be attentive to those around you, perhaps a care giver or friend. Ask them how they are doing. Tell them you care about them.

I think of the grandchild who was helping Grandpa work on his car. The grandchild would mainly watch and talk with Grandpa. Someone asked the child what Grandpa was paying him to help him with the automobile. I love what the little guy said: "Grandpa pays me attention."

You might purchase some little something for that special person this Christmas. It needn't be expensive. But I can guarantee what they will remember the most is that you came, sat down, and paid them attention.

"When people talk, listen completely. Most people never listen."
---Ernest Hemingway

Remind me Lord, that when I take time to pay attention to others, I am expressing your love to them.

Day 11
Remembering the Cross this Christmas

> *The message of the cross is foolish to those headed for destruction! But we who are being saved know it is the very power of God."---I Corinthians 1:18*

We think about the cross and what it means to us during the season of Lent; Advent focuses our attention on the birth of Christ. But Christ's birth and his death are inextricably connected. That's because apart from his birth there would have been no cross and apart from the cross, there would have been no resurrection, and his birth would have been long forgotten.

Many paintings of the nativity depict Jesus lying in a simple wooden crib in the manger. We have no way of knowing if Jesus was actually born in such a crib. But it reminds me of the close connection between the nature of Christ's birth and his death. Placed in a wooden crib at birth, he was taken from a wooden cross at his death. And neither the crib nor the cross could confine Christ.

To the Greeks of Jesus day, the idea that a god would be crucified was scandalous. Cicero, the Roman author and orator wrote that the cross, the instrument of death, should "be far away from Roman citizens, not from their bodies only, but from their thoughts, their eyes, and their ears." It would have been absurd to the mind of in the Greco/Roman world to think of a god being crucified on a cross.

In fact we get the words, "moron," and "moronic" from the very word Paul used to describe the Greco-Roman world's reaction to the cross. Both the birth and death of Christ was and is foolishness to the worldly wise.

Yet for those being saved, the Christ event is "the power of God."

Take some time to ponder the depth of what it means for Christ to come to us in the way he did. Then thank him for enduring the cross for you. Christmas means something because of the cross.

"We might be wise to follow the insight of the enraptured heart rather than the more cautious reasoning of the theological mind."

— A.W. Tozer, *The Knowledge of the Holy*

O Lord, I am amazed at how you work. May I receive you, the child born in a manger, and follow you, the man who went to the cross for me.

Day **12**

Controlling your Attitude this Christmas

> *"Let this mind be in you, which was also in Christ Jesus"---Philippians 2:5*

Christmas stresses many people. Maybe it's the crowds at the shopping malls, the parties you had just as soon skip but don't for fear of hurting someone's feelings, or perhaps it's Christmas memories---some good and some painful--that haunt you, causing that sense of lostness that you can't quite trace to its source.

It's essential that we choose to have a positive attitude before we let something or someone give us a bad one.

I saw a cartoon once that depicted a mother and daughter rushing into a department store during Christmas season. The mother is speaking to her daughter and neither is making eye contact with the other as they focus on what's ahead. The mother's wearied face reveals her frustration.

"Did you see the nasty look that clerk gave me when we walked by?' the mother snaps.

"No," the daughter answers. "I don't think she gave it to you, Mom. You already had it when you walked in."

Ultimately, we are responsible for our attitudes. If you focus on what you don't like, then you are likely to have an unpleasant attitude that shows in your demeanor. If you focus on what brings you joy, you are likely to be a more relaxed and agreeable person.

We all have to do some unpleasant things this time of year. Having a good attitude doesn't mean you hide in your room, wishing it would go away. Since most of what you don't like doing you will have to do anyway, why not bury your grumble, take charge of your attitude, and try and bring out the best in others? You'll be surprised at how much better your situation will appear.

"It isn't what you have or who you are or where you are or what you are doing that makes you happy or unhappy. It is what you think about it."

— Dale Carnegie, How to Win Friends and Influence People

Lord, thank you for reminding me that my attitude matters. As I think of your blessings today, I gently smile. Looking up to you, I sense you taking my hand and walking me through this day. How can I not be joyful?

Day 13
God can't take his eyes off you

> *How precious are your thoughts about me, O God.*
> *They cannot be numbered!* ¹⁸ *I can't even count them; they outnumber the grains of sand! And when I wake up, you are still with me!* --- (Psalm 139:17-18)

Pastor Greg Laurie tells the story about the little boy who had a reputation for misbehaving in church. One Sunday in frustration his Sunday School teacher threatened the little guy by saying, "I may not see you every time you act ugly, but God will never take his eyes off of you!"

The boy's eyes grew large and tears trickled down his cheeks. He now pictured God as a tyrant eager to punish any missteps.

On the way home from church, the boy didn't say a word. Finally as his dad drove into driveway, the boy asked what the teacher meant by his words.

Sensing a teachable moment, his mother replied, "Son, what he meant was that God loves you so much that he just can't take his eyes off of you."

And it is true, you know.

God loves us more than we can imagine.

I watch my grandson when he's at our house. I love that little guy so much it's hard for me to turn my attention away from him. But my love for him can't begin to compare to the love God has for each of us.

Some people have the mistaken notion that God is mad at them. It's true that God is a God of justice. But he is every bit as much a God of mercy. It isn't a matter of if God loves us; it's only a question of if we are willing to receive his love.

During Advent we think of the love God the Father has for us as we contemplate the mystery of how the Christ child came to us. God loves us so much that he gave his one and only Son to show us his divine love. The Holy Spirit opens our heart to that love.

You truly are amazing to God. He just can't take his eyes off you.

"God loves each of us as if there were only one of us." --- Augustine of Hippo

Father, thank you for loving me. Even now as I pray, I know you have your eyes of love on me. May I walk in your love each moment of this day.

Day **14**
A Guest in your House

> *She gave birth to her first child, a son. She wrapped him snugly in strips of cloth and laid him in a manger, because there was no lodging available for them. --- (Luke 2:7)*

Have you ever had guests that made themselves too much at home? Maybe they began rearranging things without your permission, or opened the refrigerator and ate food you had planned for another meal.

Satan is a bit like that. You invite him in for just a little while. Before you know it, you look around and he has his feet propped on your furniture, TV clicker in hand, and the oven is warming the pizza you had planned to eat. He's adjusted your thermostat to suit him, and thrown your pillow out in the hallway because he has taken over your bedroom.

Worse still, when you ask him when he plans to leave, he just laughs.

Contrast that to Jesus. He comes to us much the same way he came to Bethlehem. He doesn't intrude or force his way in. If he is not welcomed, he moves on. And once invited in, he is the perfect guest. In fact, you want him to stay because he seems to make everything better. The more you get to know him, the more authority you want him to have in your home. It doesn't take long before you no longer consider him a guest; he's the master of the house. And even though you may resist letting him have control of some rooms in your home, deep in your heart, you know what he wants is best for you.

You see, inviting him in and having fellowship with him is what following Jesus is all about.

"Jesus tapped me on the shoulder and said, Bob, why are you resisting me? I said, I'm not resisting you! He said, You gonna follow me? I said, I've never thought about that before! He said, When you're not following me, you're resisting me." --Bob Dylan

Thank you Lord, for coming into my house. I know that I am not worthy for you to come under my roof, but you came anyway and that changes everything.

Day 15
What are You Thinking?

> "And now, dear brothers and sisters, one final thing. Fix your thoughts on what is true, and honorable, and right, and pure, and lovely, and admirable. Think about things that are excellent and worthy of praise."--- (Philippians 4:8)

I love the story about the two Buddhist monks who were traveling together. They reached a river where they met a woman who was afraid to cross. She asked if they would carry her. One monk hesitated but the other agreed immediately. This monk proceeded to put her on his shoulders and transport her safely to the other side where he promptly put her down. After thanking him, she went on her way. As the monks continued to travel, the other monk seemed agitated. Finally he spoke up: "Brother, did you forget what we teach? We are not to have any contact with women, yet you just picked one up and placed her on your shoulders."

"Brother," the second monk replied, "I set her down when we reached the other side of the river. Why are you still carrying her?"

I've missed Christ too many times because I was carrying unnecessary baggage. Maybe you have too. We look at others, compare what they have to what we have, what they can purchase for Christmas and what we can't, where they can go for Christmas vacation and where we can't. The list could go on and on. In the process, we can secretly become envious, then judgmental.

What are you carrying that you need to release? What's keeping you from enjoying this moment with Christ?

Let it go and instead fix your thoughts on Christ. You'll find him coming to your aid, and you'll experience a renewed freedom to embrace life.

"The things we ruminate on, the things we insist on carrying in our minds and hearts, the things we refuse to put down...are really the things that poison us and erode our souls."
---Joan Chittister, in *Insights for the Ages*

Lord, forgive me for allowing the worries of the world to dominate my thinking. I release them to you even as I anticipate meeting you.

Day **16**

Looking unto Jesus

"Look straight ahead, and fix your eyes on what lies before you."--- (Proverbs 4:25)

When I was in high school I worked one summer on a farm. The first time I drove the tractor to plow a field, it was almost a disaster. I kept looking behind me to see how I was doing. Instead of plowing a straight line, my furrow was squiggly. My friend, whose dad was the farmer, waved his hands for me to stop. After pointing out my crooked lines, he told me to pick out some object in the distance and keep my eyes on it. "Focus on that object in front of you, not what's behind you."

I did, and it worked.

It works for life too. If you focus on what's behind you, you'll run into trouble because you aren't living in the present and will be unprepared for what's before you.

Proverbs 4:25-27 gives us clear instruction about making the most of our life. "Look straight ahead," the writer admonishes us. "Fix your eyes on what lies before you."

As you fix your eyes on what's before you, you gaze toward your ultimate goal: becoming more and more like Christ. Don't simply focus on the present for the present moment's sake or fix your eyes ahead for nothing. Paul told the Colossians: "Set your sights on the realities of heaven, where Christ sits in the place of honor at God's right hand."--- (Colossians 3:1)

As you anticipate the celebration of Christ's birth, fix your eyes heavenward, and Christ will enable you to stay faithful.

"Ponder the path of your feet," the proverb reminds us. --- (Proverbs 4:24 KJV)

As you do, looking straight ahead, plowing a straight line, you'll leave a legacy for others to follow.

"Keep your eyes on the prize."
---The title of a folk song popular among participants of the American civil rights moment during the 1950s and 1960s.

Lord, thank you that you do not leave me alone. I look to the heavens and know you are already here.

Day **17**

The Gift that Lasts

> *"Three things will last forever---faith, hope, and love---and the greatest of these is love."---I Corinthians 13:13*

I remember when I was in kindergarten, I got a football uniform one Christmas, and my brother, Mark, gave me a pair of PF Flyers to go with them.

I thought those were the two greatest gifts a kid could receive. For months, whenever we had "show and tell" at Jack and Jill Kindergarten, I would wear that uniform and those PF Flyers. I loved to zoom around in my uniform and sneakers with a football in my hands.

Believe it or not, the uniform survived so that my own son, Dave, could wear it when he was a little guy. The football helmet is at the house. The PF Flyers were lost along the way, surely worn out.

But the thing I remember most about those gifts was the joy my older brother had in watching me enjoy them. For years, he would remind me of the best Christmas present I ever received, thanks to him, of course. I can see the smile on his face even as I write these words. You see, it's the love, joy, and surprise that surround the giving and receiving that stays with us long after the gift is gone. That's what makes the gifts alive in us today, years after the giving.

God gave us the greatest gift he could give, his Son. What pleases the Father is that we receive and enjoy life with his Son. He delights in that.

Somebody said it like this: "If I could give you the best gift of all, I would give you the gift of love. This gift cannot grow old, cannot be destroyed, and even though death claims the person you love, this gift of love does not die."

Gifts fade and grow old and even get lost or misplaced. But the love in which they were given, endures forever.

It's not how much we give but how much love we put into giving."
— Mother Teresa

Thank you Father that the love of giving lasts long after the gift has disappeared.

Day **18**

One of us

> *"He appeared in human form, he humbled himself in obedience to God..."* --- *(Philippians 2:8)*

Robert Stevenson was the grandfather of the famous Scottish writer, Robert Louis Stevenson. He was a well-known engineer and builder of lighthouses. Stevenson was dearly loved by the citizens of his home town, Newcastle. To commemorate the 100th year anniversary of Stevenson's birth, Newcastle had a parade in his honor. In the procession, a farmer held a banner with the simple words, "He was one of us." Although Stevenson had received many honors for his work, those words were an affirmation of his life. Those people who knew him considered him one of them.

Jesus is King of Kings and Lord of Lords. He is the eternal Son of God. Think about it: There never was a time when he was not, but at a particular time in human history, he came to us, born in a humble stable in Bethlehem. Truly, he became "one of us."

And because he was one of us, he could live and die for us. God could have chosen to write the message of his love across the sky in big letters; he could have announced it audibly from the heavens; instead he chose to come to us as one of us.

Rest assured this Christmas that because he was one of us, he will never leave you or abandon you. He knows your deepest hurts, most shameful moments, greatest joys, and eternal hopes. He loves you as you are.

He became one of us that we might find our place with him.

Jesus Christ is not only truly God, he is human like every one of us. He is human without limitation. He is not only similar to us, he is like us." — Karl Barth, Dogmatics in Outline

It's more than I can comprehend, O Lord, to think that you became one of us. I rejoice in the knowledge that you know me just like I am and love me just the same.

Day **19**

It's Later than it's Ever Been

> *"The night is almost gone; the day of salvation will soon be here. So remove your dark deeds like dirty clothes, and put on the shining armor of right living."--- (Romans 13:12)*

A milk farmer arose each morning at four a.m. A few minutes after he was up, he would awaken his family who helped him with the milking. He was a light sleeper, so instead of setting an alarm, he listened for the old family cuckoo clock to strike four times. One day, the dirt daubers got in the clock and build their nests, causing the clock to malfunction. At midnight the clock struck twelve times, and after a pause, it started over again and struck twelve more times. The farmer bolted out of bed, ran down the hallway and shouted to his family, "Wake up, wake up, it's later than it's ever been before."

Christmas is only a few short days away. Perhaps you are like a lot of people: You still have much to do before you are ready. There are meals to prepare, gifts to purchase, social gatherings to attend, people to visit. You feel the pressure. Maybe like the farmer, you could say, "It's later than it's ever been before."

But this is a good thing, this anticipation, this final buildup before the celebration of Christmas. It can teach us to yearn for Christ, to look for him in ways we haven't before.

Maybe you can see him not only in the Christmas story but in the smile of your co-worker who is mistreated but refuses to retaliate. How about in that person who faithfully works at the soup kitchen in the homeless shelter? Could you see Christ in that person ringing the bell in front of the grocery store? How about in that elderly gentleman who sits in the back of the church praying Sunday after Sunday?

It is later than it's ever been. Christmas is near, Christ will come, even as we know he has already come, is here now, and will return.

Every year we celebrate the holy season of Advent, O God. Every year we pray those beautiful prayers of longing and waiting, and sing those lovely songs of hope and promise.
---Karl Rahner

God, I sense your presence now even as I long for you in all your fullness. You make yourself known to me in surprising ways. Help me look for you even as you have already found me.

Day **20**

Tears before Christmas

> "Weeping may last through the night, but joy comes with the morning."---(Psalm 30:5)

This particular emergency room is all too familiar to me: I know the room numbers and their location almost by memory now, having been called upon to pray here more times than I care to recall.

But every situation is a bit different; this one caught me by the throat.

I had known Colin since he was a pup, baptized him, watched him grow to young adulthood, and prayed over him when he left home on the way to fulfilling his dream of a military career.

So, that day, when I arrived at the emergency room, the news of Colin's sudden death hit me like someone had just slugged me in the stomach, knocking the wind from me. Just the week before, I had announced during Sunday's service that Colin would be home from basic training the next Sunday. "Make sure to welcome him back," I had said.

He died in a car wreck only a few miles from his house.

When I told his mom the sad news, she collapsed in my arms. A tiny measure of her pain was transfused from her heart to mine, and even that little drop of anguish was almost more than I could bear.

And so, taking a piece of her agony into mine, I cried too.

Sometime later, I can't gauge how long, I attempted a prayer. The words stuck like gravel in my throat.

I thought of Christmas, at that time only a few weeks away. How would this grieving mom make it through?

I tried praying again, hoping no one had noticed. "Keep your composure," I said to myself, repeating words I had spoken so many years ago in a football huddle when our team was in a tight spot.

The words did come, but not before tears had splashed the pages of the Scripture from which I read.

Embarrassed in the moment, I later took comfort in the thought that Jesus wept before raising Lazarus from the dead. Jesus felt the pain and didn't hide his tears.

And Mary, I am sure, cried out in pain before the joy of childbirth.

Colin's mother would make it through that Christmas, but not without tears. They were daubed by the love of Christ who would come to her through other believers, brothers and sisters bringing little respites of joy and peace.

> "I heard the bells on Christmas Day
> Their old, familiar carols play,
> And wild and sweet
> The words repeat
> Of peace on earth, good-will to men!"
> — Henry Wadsworth Longfellow

Father, I trust in you to pray through me when the pain is so great I can only pray with tears.

Day **21**

A Season for Giving

> *"You must each decide in your heart how much to give. And don't give reluctantly or in response to pressure. 'For God loves a person who gives cheerfully.'"--- (II Corinthians 9:7)*

Some people become stingy with God during the Christmas season. I suppose their reasoning is that, what with all the extra expenses at Christmas, God can wait until they can catch up on their financial shortfall. Too often, they don't.

What's sad is that the holiday designed to celebrate the birth of Jesus is for many people, anything but that.

Here's the worst part. When you make room for everything else but Christ, you really do miss out on the joy of Christmas.

As a child, I always had a feeling I had done something right when I gave part of my allowance for the Christmas missions offering. I had given to Christ, and I sensed that he was pleased with what I had done. It brought a smile to my face, and I believe God was smiling too.

As we grow older and take on more and more responsibilities, life gets more and more complicated; it's easy to miss that act of simple giving. And with it, the celebration is diminished.

Many people are in financial straits, and Christmas puts added pressure on them. I understand that. I've experienced it myself.

Here's a suggestion. Think of ways to make a difference in someone's life, and do it in the name of Christ. Try this: Look at the average price of a present you give a family member during Christmas. Think about giving a special offering for some needy person or cause in that amount.

And remember what the One whose birthday we celebrate this month once said, "When you did it to one of the least of these my brothers and sisters, you were doing it to me!"

Then, after you given, take a deep breath, smile and say, "I've just celebrated Christmas."

"This may be said of all our estates: what God gives us, is not given us for ourselves, but, 'for the Lord.'"
---Cotton Mather, *Essays to Do Good*

Help me, Lord, this day to see people as you see them and give where I can to those in need, and as I do, may I remember how unreservedly you have given to me.

Day **22**

Courageous in the Crisis

> *They were on the way up to Jerusalem, and Jesus was walking ahead of them. The disciples were filled with awe, and the people following behind were overwhelmed with fear. Taking the twelve disciples aside, Jesus once more began to describe everything that was about to happen to him.*
> *---Mark 10:32*

Even though he knew what awaited him there, Jesus was resolute in going to Jerusalem. Why? Because that's the reason he came: to give his life a ransom for many. (Mark 10:45) Jesus explained to his disciples in detail what would happen. It's a frightening picture. Jesus must have felt alone because the disciples just didn't seem to get it; they were still locked in on their idea of a Messiah, the conquering king who would set up an earthly kingdom.

Despite being misunderstood by his own people, even those closest to him, Jesus was determined to do what he had come to do. Notice Mark described Jesus as walking ahead of the disciples.

Mary must have known what would happen to her as she and Joseph made their way to Bethlehem. The whispers had already run through the rumor mill: "I never would have thought this of Joseph. And is the baby even his?"

Her story was not just unusual; it was unbelievable. But she said, "Yes," to God anyway. Mary was determined to follow her Lord: "May everything you have said about me come true," she told the angel. (Luke 1:38)

For Mary, following through with God's will meant not only saying "Yes," to the angel, but making the journey to Bethlehem. For Jesus, it meant walking the lonely road to

Jerusalem with followers who seemed to misunderstand his purpose.

What is it for you to go to your Bethlehem or Jerusalem? Continuing to love that child who rejects you? Determining to be kind to the one who has stabbed you in the back? Venturing out with a new ministry God has called you to start?

One thing is for sure: When you take a step with God, you run the risk of being misunderstood.

But faith calls us into our own Christmas story.

"Act boldly and unseen forces will come to your aid." --- Dorothea Brande

Lord, sometimes doing what I know you want me to do is frightening. But by faith I choose to travel the road to Christmas with you, trusting that you are not only in front of me as I go but beside me as well.

Day **23**
"Can't Buy Him Love"

> *"If a man tried to buy love with all his wealth, his offer would be utterly scorned."*
> ---Song of Solomon 8:7

The first year Lori and I were married, I bought her roses on the 20th of each month, the date we were married. I increased the number of roses each month, 2 for the second month, 3 for the third, until on our year anniversary I bought her a dozen roses. I jokingly told her that first year of marriage was an expensive one.

Of course, I wasn't trying to buy her love. We were after all, married. It was a joyful way of saying, "I love you." But of course, if I hadn't shown Lori I loved her in other ways, if I had neglected her, the roses would not have meant as much and may have been nothing more than something I bought from a florist, an empty expression, a sham, a display of hypocrisy. It could have descended into something I did for a show just so I could say, "Look what I did for my wife."

It's the same way with our Lord. We give special gifts to him not to win his love but to show our love for him. We give to our Lord because we love him, not so we so we can tell others and hear their approval.

Giving to our Lord should be one way we say, "I love you."

Sometimes we do something extra for our Lord. Christmas season is a wonderful time to express that extra for him. Think of some way you can let the Lord know you are in love with him. Could t be spending more time with him? Could it be spending less for yourself and more on him? Maybe it's helping someone you know is hurting.

Ask Christ to lead you to do something extra, and then be ready to listen and obey.

Remember, when you love others, you are loving Christ.

You can't buy him love, but you can give it to him.

"In the years when my parents were broke, Dad would give Mom a daisy for each year they were married." ---Donna Pizzolongo, daughter of George E. Roboni, Sr. from Tim Russert's *Wisdom of Our Fathers*

Lord, today I'm looking for some way to do something extra for you, because I love you.

Day **24**

Let Him Reign

> *May your Kingdom come soon.*
> *May your will be done on earth,*
> *as it is in heaven.* ---Matthew 6:10

The Kingdom Jesus was referring to when he delivered what we call, "The Sermon on the Mount," was the reign or rule of God in his people. The Kingdom is not necessarily something we can see, although we can be aware of the results it brings in such things as peace, justice, hope, and love.

Before Mary became pregnant with Jesus, the angel Gabriel told her Jesus would be ruler of a kingdom that would never end. He would deliver God's people as both Savior and King. The Kingdom of God was therefore central to Jesus' message.

How does the Kingdom grow within us so that we can extend it in the world around us? We must be willing to say, "Yes," to Jesus and his rule in our lives. We pray, "Thy will be done." The more we earnestly we pray like that, the larger his Kingdom becomes in our lives. We learn to say "Yes" to Jesus as we spend time with him, emptying ourselves of ourselves and taking more of him into our lives each day. As we meditate on his Word and imitate the Lord revealed to us there, we expand the Kingdom. We bring the Kingdom's message of Good News to the world around us---including the social institutions of which we are a part.

The Christ child, whose birth we soon celebrate, would one day go to the cross, and having been resurrected from the dead, guarantee that his Kingdom would always be present among his followers, and one day, upon his return as King of kings and Lord of lords, be fully realized.

"The most important need in the Christian world today is this inner truth nourished by this Spirit of contemplation: the praise and love of God, the longing for the coming of Christ, the thirst for the manifestation of God's glory, his truth, his justice, his Kingdom in the world."
---Thomas Merton

Lord, I yearn for you today. I intend to say "Yes," to your rule in my life. Forgive me when I forget and foolishly attempt to establish my own reign in my life.

Day **25**

Unaware of His Presence

> *"Surely the Lord was in this place, and I wasn't even aware of it."---Genesis 28:16*

We were in Mexico City. It was too difficult for my mother to stay at home that first Christmas without Dougie, my older brother by 21 months.

He had been killed in a car accident the previous May, on the last day of school. I still have his book satchel, a homemade one before the days of book bags. Having completed the first grade that day, he skipped home from Washington Elementary School, happy to be officially a 2nd grader. And tucked to one side of the satchel is his report card, signed by Mom, Mrs. L. D. Whitlock, every six weeks-- with the lone exception of that last six weeks, left blank forever.

And I, being one grade behind him, was on that day as most other school days, anxiously waiting for him to get home so we could play.

And that was the last day I saw my brother alive.

I don't remember much about that first Christmas without him. I did break a piñata, but I don't recall opening presents or seeing a Santa. It was like we were in a dream, a sad one. Though I was a six year old child with eager eyes and ears anticipating each Christmas, that Christmas didn't seem like Christmas. I missed the familiar surroundings and traditions of Christmas.

Most of all, I missed Dougie.

As I think about it, that was probably one of the most authentic Christmases I ever experienced. After all, the very first Christmas went largely unnoticed by most people, people who had hurts, and fears, people needing hope, people longing for a Messiah who would deliver them.

But Jesus was there in Bethlehem, though few knew him for who he was.

And he was in Mexico City too, albeit unbeknownst to me. Though he did not show up with fanfare, he did show up, there among the wounded---my grieving mother and father, and my older brothers, Mark and Lowell. And he was with me too, a confused little boy trying to make sense out of why my best friend, my brother, wasn't allowed to be with us that Christmas.

Jesus passes by me today, much as he did then, in ways I often don't recognize until years later when I see from a distance that he was up to something special, even though I'm not always sure what it was.

"Infinite, and infant. Eternal, and yet born of a woman. Almighty, and yet hanging on a woman's breast. Supporting a universe, and yet, needing to be carried in a mother's arms. King of angels, and yet the reputed son of Joseph. Heir of all things, and yet the carpenter's despised son."
---C.H. Spurgeon

My Lord and my God, thank you for being there, even though I didn't know it.

Day **26**

Christmas: Different, but Always the Same

> "Oh how my soul praises the Lord. How my
> spirit rejoices in God my Savior!" ---Luke 1:46

I remember the first time we flocked a Christmas tree. I couldn't have been more than nine or ten. At first I didn't like that new tree. It was different from the ones we had before.

I watched wide-eyed as Dad worked hard spraying the white "flocking" over the tree. Then we carefully moved it into our den. Where was the fresh smell of cedar? It looked like fake snow. And the decorations became more elaborate with the flocked tree. We had used simpler ones on the other trees: a few lights, stringed silver mistletoe, some ornaments.

But then, the presents were placed one by one under the flocked tree, just like we had done with the simpler trees. And I had the same anticipation: What's in those gifts? And after a few years, the smell of flocking meant Christmas was near.

The tree in my home today is neither flocked nor naturally green. It's completely artificial. But, just like those other trees, the presents gather under it. Staring at the wrapped gifts, I still wonder what's in each one (My wife does most of the wrapping), curious what each package hides, though not with the same excitement I had as a child.

Christmas trees and their decorations change through the years. The presents are different too, of course, unless you are one to re-gift.

Today I stare at the Christmas tree that I will soon box up and put back in the garage for another year. It reminds me that if Christmas is Christmas, it must remain the same, even though our traditions like decorating the tree change.

Jesus Christ is the same yesterday, today, and forever. It's in the celebrating of his birth that I find the true, unchanging, everlasting Christmas.

And it that, I can always rejoice.

Even if there is no tree or presents.

"He who has not Christmas in his heart will never find it under a tree."
---Roy L. Smith

I am grateful, Lord, that you are beyond change. May I learn something new about you every day.

Day **27**

A Gift Just for You

> *Even before he made the world, God loved us and chose us in Christ to be holy and without fault in his eyes. God decided in advance to adopt us into his own family by bringing us to himself through Jesus Christ.*
> ---Ephesans 1:4-5

In high school I worked in a men's clothing store. I was terrible at gift wrapping. Maybe it was because I was impatient or just plain clumsy. I used to pray that the wrapping paper would stay on the package until the customer made it out the door. I'm sure many required rewrapping before Christmas arrived.

God took a lot more care in preparing your Christmas present than I did with those packages. Jesus came perfectly wrapped in swaddling clothes. Jesus, the best gift ever, came to show us the Father's love. Because he was from eternity the very Son of God---fully God and completely human---he could save us from ourselves, from our sin.

As you enter into a relationship with him whereby you claim him as your only Savior, you freely receive his grace--grace sufficient to make you into all you were ever meant to be. Jesus is the whole package: Savior, Master, Redeemer, Restorer, Healer.

If you haven't already, receive that gift and enjoy Christmas.

Claim your Christmas gift from God: Jesus Christ your Savior. This gift has been prepared for you before the creation of the world.

"Christmas is based on an exchange of gifts, the gift of God to man – His unspeakable gift of His Son, and the gift of man to God – when we present our bodies a living sacrifice."
---Vance Havner

O God, how can I ever let you know how grateful I am for the perfect present, Jesus Christ, my Savior and Lord? All I can do is give you my life as an expression of my love.

Day **28**

Is it Over Already?

> *For a child is born to us, a son is given to us. The government will rest on his shoulders. And he will be called: Wonderful Counselor, Mighty God, Everlasting Father, and Prince of Peace. His government and its peace will never end.*
> *---Isaiah 9:6-7*

I recall a cartoon of a child surrounded by gifts he had just unwrapped on Christmas morning. The little guy is crying, and the caption reads, "Is it over already?"

Maybe you too are having a post-Christmas let down before Christmas day is even over. Perhaps you didn't get what you wanted for Christmas. Maybe it doesn't have anything to do with gifts: It could be that your loved ones have returned home and you're once again lonely. Or maybe they've stayed too long, and you're frazzled. Perhaps you're feeling melancholic because you're exhausted from doing so much to get ready for Christmas.

The after-Christmas doldrums can come from a variety of sources.

Those feelings are normal, so if you have them, don't worry too much about it, unless they linger for weeks and months.

It's always helped me, whenever I've had a post-Christmas slump, to have something more to anticipate. Lori and I have a tradition of getting away, just the two of us, for New Year's. Christmas is an especially busy time for a minister, and we've found it necessary for our mental and physical health to get away. Every Christmas I look forward to that time.

Try doing something different, something you enjoy. You don't have to leave town. You might spend some time with someone you enjoy, or take some time just to yourself.

Give yourself permission to pamper yourself by doing something *you* enjoy doing. You'll be better able to love others when you love and take care of yourself.

As you do, rejoice in what God did for you in sending his one and only Son, Jesus Christ. Spend some time thinking about all that he has done on your behalf. You might start with the material things he has provided, but remember the spiritual blessings too.

Isaiah prophesied about an everlasting Kingdom. Jesus inaugurated it when he was born; it will be fully realized when he returns. And that is truly something worth anticipating.

As we pass the love of Jesus to others, we continue to celebrate Christmas.

The joy of Christmas lasts far beyond Christmas Day. We can celebrate it throughout the year, for after all, even though we may doubt it at times, Jesus will show up.

Always.

Just in time.

And when he does, it's Christmas all over again.

"Christmas, my child, is love in action. Every time we love, every time we give, it's Christmas."
---Dale Evans

As I celebrate your birth today, Lord Jesus, let me take the joy of today into every day of the year. And when I stray, or become downcast by the struggles of the day, gently remind me that every day is Christmas because you are within, around, behind, and before me. You truly are there for me, always, just in time.

www.ingramcontent.com/pod-product-compliance
Lightning Source LLC
Chambersburg PA
CBHW050204130526
44591CB00034B/2117